CRITICAL DEBATES

The Debate About
Terrorist Tactics

DAVID SMITH

New York

Published in 2008 by The Rosen Publishing Group, Inc.
29 East 21st Street, New York, NY 10010

First Edition

Editor: Patience Coster
Series editor: Jennifer Schofield
Consultant: Madeleine Colvin
Designer: Rita Storey
Picture researcher: Diana Morris

Picture acknowledgments: Cover photograph: The remains of a bus blown apart by a suicide
bomber during the morning rush hour in central London on 7 July 2005 (Getty Images News)

The author and publisher would like to thank the following for allowing their pictures to be
reproduced in this publication: Sean Adair/Reuters/Corbis: 4; Lynsey Addario/Corbis: 33, 34, 42;
AP/Topham: 7, 11, 13, 24; Sabah Arar/Rex Features: 45; David Bathgate/Corbis: 37; Bettmann/Corbis:
8, 15, 18; Greg Bos/Reuters/Corbis: 36; Matt Dunham/Reuters/
Corbis: 31; Fujifotos/Image Works/Topfoto: *title page* and 22; Monika Graff/Image Works/Topfoto:
32; Ian Hodgson/Reuters/ Corbis: 44; James Horton/Topfoto: 23; Hulton-Deutsch Collection/Corbis:
30; Marilyn Humphries/Image Works/Topfoto: 26; Attar Maher/Sygma/Corbis: 38; George
Mulala/Reuters/Corbis: 25; Tony O'Brien/ Image Works/Topfoto: 19; PA/Topham: 12, 29;
Photri/Topham: 10, 14; Picturepoint/ Topham: 16, 17, 20; Reuters/Corbis: 36; Oswaldo
Rivas/Reuters/Corbis: 28; Jorge Silva/Reuters/Corbis: 9; Sipa Press/Rex Features: 35; Topfoto: 6; Peter
Turnley/ Corbis: 41; Teun Voeten/Image Works/Topfoto: 40.

Library of Congress Cataloging-in-Publication Data

Downing, David, 1946-
  The debate about terrorist tactics / David Downing.
      p. cm. -- (Ethical debates)
  Includes index.
  ISBN-13: 978-1-4042-3757-5 (library binding)
  ISBN-10: 1-4042-3757-7 (library binding)
  1. Terrorism--Moral and ethical aspects--Juvenile literature. 2. War on Terrorism, 2001--Moral and
ethical aspects--Juvenile literature. 3. Human rights--Juvenile literature. I. Title.
  HV6431.D673 2007
  363.325--dc22

                                    2007009499

Manufactured in China

contents

Two deaths among many

This real-life case study highlights some of the issues that surround the debate on terrorism.

case study

Two deaths among many

On the morning of September 11, 2001, 19 Islamic militant terrorists hijacked four crowded airliners that had just left Boston, Washington, DC and Newark, New Jersey. The two flights from Boston were flown into New York City's World Trade Center, setting both its towers on fire and causing them to collapse. The flight from Washington, DC was flown into the side of the Pentagon building, the headquarters of the U.S. Department of Defense. The intended target of the Newark airliner is suspected to have been the White House or the Capitol, but the aircraft was brought down in the Pennsylvania countryside by passenger resistance. In 80 minutes, 19 terrorists had killed themselves and nearly 3,000 other people. After these incidents, the attacks became known simply by the day's date—9/11.

Muhammad Atta was the 33-year-old Egyptian leader of the hijackers. All 19 men belonged to an Islamic militant organization called al-Qaeda. Atta believed that Muslims, particularly Middle Eastern Muslims, were suffering from centuries of oppression by Western powers. He believed that Islam was being undermined and insulted by Western

attitudes and values. He also believed that violence was the only way to rid the Middle East of Western political and military influence, and that terrorism was the best weapon available. He was ready to kill and die for these beliefs.

Joanne Ahladiotis was a 27-year-old Greek-American woman working on the 104th floor of the World Trade Center's North Tower. She had gone to work that morning completely unaware that she was living her final hours. She may well have had her own views about U.S. policy in the Middle East. Her friends and family may have known what these were, but Muhammad Atta and the other 18 hijackers certainly did not. She and almost 3,000 others were not killed because of anything they had done. They were killed to make a point.

Terrorism has been practiced throughout history, though rarely on the scale of 9/11. In the years that have passed since Muhammad Atta flew the hijacked airliner into Joanne Ahladiotis's workplace, terrorism has continued to claim lives in many parts of the world. In this book, we will look at how terrorists and antiterrorists have sought to justify their actions, and what their opponents have made of these arguments.

Terrorism in the twenty-first ▶
century: it is 9:03 a.m.
on the morning of
September 11, 2001.
The South Tower of the
World Trade Center bursts
into flames seconds after
being struck by United
Airlines Flight 175.
The North Tower (on the
right) is already burning,
having been struck
18 minutes earlier by
American Airlines Flight 11.
The South Tower collapsed
at 10:05 a.m., the North
Tower at 10:28 a.m.

v i e w p o i n t s

"When you board the plane, remember
that this is a battle in the sake of God,
which is worth the whole world and all
that is in it . . . And when zero-hour
comes, open your chest and welcome
death in the cause of God . . ."
From a letter carried by each group of the
9/11 hijackers

"Across the globe yesterday millions of
people stood, united in silence. Their
heads were bowed. The only sounds were
those of muffled sobs; the only movement
was the discreet raising of hands to wipe
away the tears."
Paul Vallely, reporting for the *Independent*
newspaper on the three-minute silence
held for the victims of the 9/11 attacks.
An estimated 800 million people observed
the silence in 43 countries.

CHAPTER 1

Different kinds of terrorism

Since human life began, people have tried to terrorize others in order to achieve what they want. Individual leaders and governments have terrorized their followers and peoples for almost as long. The word *terrorism* was first used in the late eighteenth century to describe the actions of the revolutionary government in France. In 1793–4, this government scared its opponents into submission by executing around 4,000 of them in what became known as the "Reign of Terror." A year later, the *Oxford English Dictionary* included the word "terrorism" for the first time, defining it as "government by intimidation, as directed and carried out by the party in power."

▼ Tsar Alexander II of Russia is assassinated by a suicide bomber in St Petersburg in 1881.

By the end of the nineteenth century, this definition was clearly out of date. By this point, terrorism was generally considered to be a tactic used *against* governments, not *by* them. Terrorists were people who used bombs or bullets to assassinate leading political figures, such as Tsar Alexander II of Russia in 1881 or the Austrian Archduke Franz Ferdinand in June 1914. The aim of terrorism was to terrorize governments into changing their policies.

The years between the two world wars saw both types in operation. Antigovernment violence was still considered terrorism, but so was the deliberate terrorizing of whole populations by dictatorial governments. The Soviet and Nazi German governments both made extensive use of terror against real and potential internal opponents.

Civilian targets

During World War II (1939–45), a new form of terrorism took hold. It consisted of aerial bombing attacks against civilian populations with the intention of terrifying them into submission. Both sides carried out such attacks: the Germans against people living in British cities, and the British and U.S. air forces, who killed hundreds of thousands of German and Japanese civilians in conventional—and eventually nuclear—attacks.

Aerial bombing of civilian targets has rarely been called terrorism by those who practice it. After World War II, the word "terrorist" was reserved, once again, for those who used violence against governments—but with one big difference. When the Cold War began in 1947, the opposing sides directed violence against each other, and both sides described the military allies of their opponents as terrorists. Their own military allies, however, were usually described as "freedom fighters."

▲ A street in London's East End following a massive German bombing attack on September 8, 1940. The principal intention of raids like this, which killed many civilians, was to terrify the population.

viewpoints

"The terrorist is noble, terrible, irresistibly fascinating, for he combines in himself . . . the martyr and the hero. From the day he swears in the depths of his heart to free the people and the country, he knows he is consecrated to death. He goes forth to meet it fearlessly . . . "
Serge Stepniak-Kravchinski,
Underground Russia, 1883

"In the terrorists, evil has found a willing servant."
President George W. Bush,
October 11, 2001

▲ Red Brigades members Adriana Faranda and Valerio Morucci wait behind bars in a Rome courtroom in 1984. They were on trial for the suspected kidnap and murder of Italian politician, Aldo Moro in 1978.

Terrorism in recent times

Over the last half century, those using terrorism have fallen into three main categories. The first and least important of these was the handful of tiny, extreme left-wing groups that appeared in Europe and North America during the late 1960s and early 1970s. The Baader-Meinhof group in Germany, the Red Brigades in Italy, and the Weathermen in the U.S. were prominent examples. All these groups used terrorism, mostly bombings, kidnappings, and shootings, as their primary tactic. Their objective was the complete overthrow of the existing socioeconomic system, which they considered both heartless and unjust. These groups had few members and few supporters, and failed to achieve their aims.

Governments made up the second category. When terrorist groups are trained, armed, and funded by governments, this is known as *state-sponsored terrorism*. During the Cold War, the U.S. and Soviet Union trained the other side's enemies in terrorist techniques and sponsored terrorist operations. Sometimes states use terrorist tactics themselves, known as *state terrorism*. Both Cold War superpowers employed what some would call state terrorism in their own wars, most notably in Vietnam and Afghanistan. Many other governments have used similar tactics against particular sections of their own people. In the 1990s, for example, Indian governments subjected the people of Kashmir to random arrests and the routine use of torture. The Guatemalan government of the 1980s used death squads to torture and murder its Native American population. The Serbian government in Bosnia used mass rape to terrify its Muslim population. During the past 50 years, government or state terrorism has been responsible for the vast majority of terrorism's victims.

The third category includes individuals and groups fighting against various forms of foreign rule and occupation. In most such cases, terrorism has been adopted because the groups or individuals believed that neither military confrontation nor democratic politics offered any real hope of dislodging the oppressor. The Irish Republican Army (IRA) in Northern Ireland, the Basque ETA group in northeast Spain, and the Tamil Tigers in Sri Lanka are three prominent examples. All of these groups have used other tactics, but terrorism has been their preferred method.

Since the early 1980s, terrorists inspired by an extreme interpretation of Islam have created their own subcategory. Groups like al-Qaeda, which launched the 9/11 attacks against the U.S., believed that the Middle East was occupied by richer Western countries and local pro-Western governments. Terrorism was the tactic these groups chose to drive the Westerners out.

It's a fact

Suicide attacks, in which attackers sacrifice their own lives in order to kill others, have a long history. In recent times, the tactic has mostly been used by Islamic militants, who call such attacks "martyrdom operations." By dying for their religion, they expect to secure places in paradise.

▼ In 2001, Guatemalan Native Americans re-bury the victims of earlier state-sponsored terrorism. In recent years, almost 700 mass graves have been discovered, dating from the 1970s and 1980s.

The War on Terror

Within days of the 9/11 attacks, President George W. Bush announced a "War on Terror." Unsurprisingly, the war's first targets were the Afghanistan-based al-Qaeda leaders who were believed to have been responsible for planning and financing the attacks. When the local Taliban government refused to hand the suspects over, a U.S.-led military force went in to Afghanistan to find them. The Taliban was overthrown, and the al-Qaeda leaders were forced into hiding.

President Bush then went on to describe his other targets in the War on Terror. "Our war begins with al-Qaeda," he said on September 20, 2001, "but it does not end there." A month later he told journalists: "So long as anybody is terrorizing established governments, there needs to be a war." Terrorism, in other words, had been redefined as any violent activity directed against lawful governments. Critics were quick to point out that such a definition meant that American heroes, such as George Washington, would be included among the list of terrorists.

The War on Terror continued on many fronts. In Afghanistan, soldiers scoured the most remote hills for signs of the missing al-Qaeda leaders. Intelligence and security services around the world were involved in tracking sympathizers and potential recruits, and in seeking out information that would enable them to prevent future attacks. Financial institutions froze bank accounts of people and organizations that were believed to be supporters of terrorism, and tightened their rules to remove sources of funding. New laws, rules, and procedures were introduced which made it easier to arrest, detain, and question those suspected of involvement in terrorism.

▲ U.S. forces search a village in the Kandahar province of Afghanistan in March 2003. Although the Taliban government was overthrown in November 2001, many of its leaders and supporters are still active in the southern regions of the country.

Into Iraq

The next military target of the War on Terror was highly controversial. The reasons given for the invasion of Iraq—that Saddam Hussein's government had been producing weapons of mass destruction (WMD) and was likely to pass them on to al-Qaeda-style terrorists—proved false. No WMD were found. Opponents argued that the invasion of Iraq was undertaken for different reasons (see pages 42–3), and that the War on Terror was being used as a convenient excuse.

Other governments around the world were also using President Bush's wide definition of terrorism to deal with internal opponents. For example, the Russian and Israeli governments quickly announced that their long-running wars with the Chechens and Palestinians were part of the War on Terror. Both the Chechens and the Palestinians have used terrorism during their struggles, alongside other tactics. Some people have argued that dismissing them as terrorists makes it easier for the Russians and Israelis to ignore the real grievances behind those struggles. But equally, it can be argued that if a group terrorizes and kills innocent civilians, whether or not it uses other more peaceful tactics as well, people will understandably label it a terrorist organization. A group would need to renounce violence altogether to free itself of this label.

It's a fact

Weapons of mass destruction (WMD) comprise nuclear weapons, modern biological weapons (such as specially manufactured viruses or germs), and modern chemical weapons (such as nerve gases). Since these weapons can kill large numbers of people very quickly, their possible use by terrorists is a major source of concern.

▼ In Grozny, the capital city of Chechnya, women protest against the Russian re-conquest of their region in December 1994.

Firemen search for victims in the rubble of an IRA bomb attack in Birmingham, U.K., on November 21, 1974.

Defining terrorism

A simple definition of terrorism is that it is the use of violence against civilians, especially for political ends. However, there are some problems with this definition. Its three main ingredients—violence, civilians, and political ends—are all open to interpretation. Is stone throwing, for example, violent enough to qualify? Do political leaders count as civilians? What exactly are political ends? There are no clear-cut answers to any of these questions, but common sense can usually be applied. Blowing up a dictator in pursuit of democracy is clearly an act of terrorism, even if the political end might seem beneficial. Throwing a punch at a passer-by during an environmental demonstration is clearly not, because it is a random act of violence without an obvious political motive.

Nevertheless, this definition makes it clear that there are crucial distinctions. Terrorists can be individuals, groups, or governments. Attacks that target civilians are terrorist attacks, wherever, whenever, and by whoever, they are carried out. A bomb left on a commuter train, a bomb

case study

The men and women of the IRA

Between the late 1960s and 1997, Irish nationalists in Northern Ireland mounted a campaign to drive out the British. The most powerful nationalist group, the Irish Republican Army, or IRA, used many different tactics. Some, like political campaigning and the use of hunger strikes for propaganda purposes, were essentially peaceful. Many IRA activities, however, involved the use of violence.

This violence came in two basic forms. IRA men and women attacked individual British soldiers and British military positions; they planted bombs in ordinary urban locations with the intention of scaring or killing civilians and shocking the public and the government. Successive British governments considered these men and women to be terrorists, and called the IRA a terrorist organization. The IRA considered both forms of violence to be legitimate tactics of resistance.

According to the definition of terrorism given on this page, both were wrong. The attacks on military targets were either crimes or acts of war, depending on whether or not one accepted Britain's right to rule part of Ireland. The killings of civilians were acts of terrorism.

dropped from an aircraft on a sleeping city—both can be seen as acts of terrorism.

The bombing of an occupying army's barracks, an aerial strike against rebel

◀ In 1983, a casualty of a bomb attack on U.S. Marine barracks in the Lebanese capital, Beirut, is carried away. More than 200 people were killed in the attack.

summary

▶ Terrorism is a weapon sometimes used by people who feel their rights, desires, or interests are being denied by their own government or a foreign government. Such people believe that the use of terrorist tactics is their best hope of changing this situation.

▶ Terrorism can be used by governments or individuals to try to force their will on others.

viewpoints

"The reports reveal that eight Israeli State terrorists were killed and another seven were injured. Members of the Lebanese resistance bombarded Israeli towns and settlements in northern Israel with more than 80 Katyusha rockets."
The Palestine Free Voice website, claiming that all Israelis are "state terrorists"

"Everyone remaining in southern Lebanon will be regarded as a terrorist, Israel's justice minister said yesterday as the military prepared to employ 'huge firepower' from the air in its campaign to crush Hezbollah."
The *Daily Telegraph* website on July 28, 2006, where an Israeli government spokesman claimed that all Lebanese are "terrorists"

soldiers—these are not acts of terrorism. Attacks on military targets may be considered good or bad moves strategically, depending on the situation; but, since they are not aimed at civilians, most people would not see them as terrorist attacks.

Terrorist tactics in wartime

There is a long history of terrorist acts in wars between two or more states. In the late fourteenth century, the Mongol leader, Tamurlane, liked to leave a mound of skulls where a defiant city had been. This spread fear, and helped to make the next city easier to conquer. In World War II, German units executed batches of civilian hostages for each German soldier killed by resistance fighters. They wanted the civilian population to be afraid of helping the resistance.

Airborne tactics

Such acts of military terrorism are explicitly prohibited by internationally accepted conventions covering the activities of armies in wartime, and few attempts are made to justify them. However, airborne campaigns that some people would consider to be terrorism

viewpoints

"I am therefore addressing this urgent appeal to every government . . . that its armed forces shall in no event, and under no circumstances, undertake the bombardment from the air of civilian populations or of unfortified cities."
President Franklin D. Roosevelt, speaking on September 1, 1939

"There seems little doubt that this would break the spirit of the German people."
From a 1942 British government report on the benefits of bombing German cities

▼ An Iraqi government building burns following a coalition air attack in April 2003. U.S. and British forces in Iraq made extensive use of their superior air power.

have been harder to stop. Aerial bombing of civilian targets was a major feature of World War II, killing over a million civilians, and has subsequently been used in Vietnam, Afghanistan, and Iraq. Such bombing is intended, among other things, to terrorize. One U.S. bombing campaign on Baghdad, Iraq, in 2003 was called "Shock and Awe." It was intended to stun the enemy into submission, but without causing civilian casualties owing to the use of precision-guided bombs aimed only at government and military targets. In fact, although most of the strikes were surgical, there were some civilian casualties.

Supporters claim that aerial bombing weakens civilian morale and lessens civilian support for continuing the war. This, they say, puts pressure on governments to surrender or seek peace, thus shortening wars and actually saving lives. Opponents have two basic arguments against the bombing of civilians. First, that killing noncombatants is wrong in itself. Second, that it is usually counterproductive. There is much evidence to show that British, German, and North Vietnamese civilian morale was stiffened by the bombing these countries endured.

case study

Akihiro Takahashi

In early August 1945, the U.S. dropped two atomic bombs on the Japanese cities of Hiroshima and Nagasaki, killing around 220,000 civilians. Those who ordered these attacks claimed that they were trying to save American lives by making an invasion of Japan unnecessary.

Akihiro Takahashi was 14 years old and standing in line outside his school when the first bomb exploded. "Everything collapsed for as far as I could see . . . I looked at myself and found my clothes had turned into rags due to the heat . . . my skin was peeling and hanging . . ."

The intention of the bombings had been to terrify the Japanese into surrendering. In the eyes of their opponents, the more terrified they were, the better. Some people consider these two bombings to be the greatest acts of terrorism in history.

▼ An aerial view of the devastated city of Hiroshima, Japan, after the U.S. atomic bomb attack at the end of World War II.

▲ In Saigon in 1968, a South Vietnamese soldier sits amid the rubble following the bombardment of his city. During the civil war in Vietnam, heavy military attacks such as this were combined with the use of terrorist and guerrilla tactics. The war continued for many years as the violence escalated on both sides.

Civil wars

In wars between states, civilian populations have usually supported their own governments and armies. There has rarely been any doubt of their loyalty. In civil wars, however, the loyalty of the civilian population to one side or the other has usually been the crucial factor. Civil wars are as much about "winning hearts and minds" as they are about winning military battles. Enormous efforts are put into persuading people of the rightness of the conflicting causes.

Such persuasion can be friendly. It can involve argument, propaganda, even bribery. However, persuasion through fear has often played a significant part. During the Vietnamese civil war (1945–75), the communist Vietcong rebels killed hundreds of pro-government village headmen as a means of strengthening their own authority and frightening off potential opponents. During the civil war in British-ruled Palestine in 1947–8, the inhabitants of an Arab village named Deir

Yassin were massacred by members of a Jewish terrorist group, at least partly with the intention of scaring other Arabs from their own villages. In the Afghan civil war of the early 1990s, some Islamic militant groups began murdering female teachers. Women were afraid to take such jobs, which slowed the drive for reform and weakened the communist government's authority.

In all of these three civil wars, both sides committed terrorist acts. The terrorists who committed the acts all proved victorious. They argued afterward that such acts had been necessary to ensure their victories, and that victory for their cause—a unified communist Vietnam, the establishment of a Jewish state, the defeat of communism in Afghanistan—justified their use of terrorism. In their view, the end had justified the means.

The two arguments used against terrorism in wars between states can also be applied to terrorism in civil wars. The deliberate killing of civilians is unacceptable, whatever the circumstances, and can seem even crueller when the civilians in question are fellow citizens. Terrorism is also counterproductive. Although terrorists may sometimes achieve their political aims, the use of terrorism can leave societies with a legacy of violence and bitterness that can take generations to overcome. There are always other, nonviolent methods of achieving political aims that can be just as effective in the long run.

▼ A truck loaded with explosives is detonated by Jewish terrorists on Jerusalem's Ben-Jehuda Street in February 1948.

Resisting occupation

During wars between several states, some defeated countries may be occupied by the armies of those still fighting. In World War II, for example, France, Poland, Greece, and Czechoslovakia were among the countries occupied by the Germans. Resistance movements were formed in each of these countries to fight the occupation. Terrorism was one of the tactics they used.

These resistance groups did not recognize any difference between the soldiers sent to occupy their countries and the civilians sent to govern them. They attacked both military and civilian targets. In 1942, Reinhard Heydrich, the German governor of Bohemia and Moravia (those parts of Czechoslovakia ruled by Germany between 1939 and 1945), was assassinated by Czechoslovakian resistance fighters, who had been trained in Britain. This was clearly an act of terrorism. So, too, was the shooting of German civilian administrators in Paris, Warsaw, and Athens during the war. Such attacks were supposed to scare the Germans, and make them less effective as occupiers.

It's a fact

The Nazi authorities falsely described all resistance as terrorism, making no distinction between attacks on civilian and military targets. Their punishment of resisters was often equally terroristic. Most of the men, women, and children in Lidice (Czechoslovakia), Oradour-sur-Glane (France), and Kortelisy (Ukraine), for example, were massacred in response to acts of resistance.

▼ This boy is one of seven people to survive the Nazi slaughter at the village of Oradour-sur-Glane, France, in 1944. He stands before a mass grave containing the bodies of many of the 740 other villagers.

▲ Resistance fighters of the Jammu and Kashmir Liberation Front (JKLF)
pose for the camera in June 1993. The JKLF seeks to establish Kashmir
as a state independent of both India and Pakistan.

Resistance groups also used terrorism against their fellow citizens. Like the occupiers, resistance groups tried to terrify the passive civilian majority into supporting—or at least not opposing—their aims. Many men and women who collaborated with the occupiers were executed, partly to scare others out of doing the same.

During the war, the Germans frequently criticized the terrorist tactics used by resistance movements. After the war, the word "terrorist" was rarely used to describe these tactics. Many felt that the collaborators had only themselves to blame for having chosen the wrong side. The men who killed Heydrich—one of the main organizers of the Holocaust—were regarded more as heroes than terrorists.

Had a troubling precedent been set? World War II was the last long war between states in which countries were occupied for years on end. However, several short wars have given way to long occupations. For example, in the view of some commentators, India has been illegally occupying part of Kashmir for almost 60 years. Israel has occupied the Palestinian West Bank and Gaza Strip since 1967, and the Russians have been in Chechnya since the late eighteenth century. Are resistance movements in these regions as justified in their use of terrorism as the resistance movements in World War II were?

summary

▶ Those people who believe that terrorist tactics can be justified in wartime argue that this is because they weaken civilian morale, shorten wars (thus saving lives), and contribute to victory.

▶ Those who believe that it is not possible to justify terrorist tactics in wartime argue that this is because it is morally wrong to kill civilians, and because killing them often strengthens morale, makes wars longer, and ultimately leads to defeat.

Terrorist tactics in peacetime

Many activities that seem tolerable in wartime: the killing of fellow human beings, for example, have always been considered less tolerable in peacetime. In recent years, however, the line between war and peace has become increasingly blurred. Wars are rarely declared, and often have no formal ending. If territory has changed hands, its status remains unresolved. Although open warfare may have ceased, those who have been occupied still feel that it is their duty to resist their occupation.

viewpoints

"If the question is, is it possible to bring about liberation by means of terror? The answer is: No! If the question is, do these actions help to bring liberation nearer? The answer is: Yes!"
From a Jewish Lehi group publicity sheet, 1943; the Lehi group used terrorist tactics to fight for the formation of a Jewish state in Palestine

"What we can be slightly more sure about is that the use of the tactic of terror by a terrorist group will invariably be ill-advised, at least for reasons of inefficacy, if not also for reasons of immorality."
Conor Gearty, *The Future of Terrorism*, 1999

▼ At Dawson's Field in Jordan on September 12, 1970, one of three hijacked aircraft has just been blown up by members of the Popular Front for the Liberation of Palestine (PFLP). The explosion sends a thick cloud of black smoke into the desert sky.

In the early twenty-first century, most of the inhabitants of the Palestinian West Bank and Gaza Strip, Indian Kashmir, Chechnya, and Iraq consider themselves to be occupied by a foreign power or powers. How can they bring political pressure to bear on their occupiers? Is direct military confrontation possible? Or should they mount surprise attacks against political, economic, and military targets? If none of these is possible, then they may resort to violent attacks on civilians—in other words, terrorism.

Do such attacks force the occupier to reconsider the occupation? This has not often happened. However, the success of two terrorist campaigns against the British—by Jewish groups in Palestine (1945–7) and Irish nationalists in Northern Ireland (1972–97)—suggests that the use of terrorism may persuade governments to change their policies.

▼ Palestinian president Yasser Arafat argues a point with President Bill Clinton during the July 2000 Middle East peace talks held in the U.S.

case study

Yasser Arafat

Yasser Arafat was a Palestinian nationalist who spent his life struggling to win a homeland for his people. Over the course of half a century, he used many different tactics in pursuit of this goal. After Israel's establishment in 1948, he hoped that the armies of the Arab states would win back the Palestinians' land. When it became clear, with the Arab defeat in 1967, that this was not going to happen, Arafat became a guerrilla fighter in the occupied territories. When this failed, he supported, or at least failed to condemn, the use of terrorist tactics. These tactics won publicity for his cause, but little else, and in the 1980s he turned to diplomacy. He helped to negotiate a peace deal with Israel in 1993 that allowed the Palestinians limited self-rule; but by the early 2000s, with the peace process stalled, Arafat was accused by Israel of secretly supporting terrorist attacks. Arafat died in 2004, remaining a controversial figure to the end. To some, he was a heroic freedom fighter and symbol of Palestinian national aspirations, but to his opponents, he was never more than a terrorist.

Domestic terrorism in peacetime

Terrorism has not been restricted to conflicts involving different ethnic or religious groups. People have used terrorist attacks against their own governments, and governments have used terrorist tactics against sections of their own people.

The Red Brigades in Italy and the Baader-Meinhof group in Germany launched terrorist campaigns in the 1970s, kidnapping and murdering businessmen and politicians. The communist guerrillas of the Peruvian Shining Path were responsible in the 1980s and 1990s for multiple bombings and the murder of numerous civilian administrators.

In March 1995, members of a religious sect called Aum Shinrikyo released Sarin nerve gas in the Tokyo subway, killing 12 people. It was later discovered that the sect had enough Sarin to kill four million people. The next month, a Gulf War veteran named Timothy McVeigh detonated a bomb outside a federal government building in Oklahoma City, killing 167 people.

A means to what end?

What did these terrorists expect to gain from their acts? The European groups and the Peruvian Shining Path hoped to overthrow global capitalism. Aum Shinrikyo's motives have never been revealed. Timothy McVeigh wanted to bring down the United States' federal

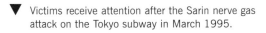

▼ Victims receive attention after the Sarin nerve gas attack on the Tokyo subway in March 1995.

▲ A Chilean woman holds up a picture of her "disappeared" uncle during an anti-Pinochet protest in London, U.K., in October 1998.

government. Since the intended "ends" of all these attacks were either unachievable or unstated, they could hardly be used to justify the murderous means. Futhermore, in all four cases, terrorism was far from the last resort. Unlike the Chechens, Kashmiris, or Palestinians (see page 19), all of these terrorists had the opportunity to influence events through a democratic process—in other words, by using their vote at election time.

Despite its origins in the French Revolution, the word "terrorist" has rarely been used to describe governments. Even the Soviet and Nazi dictatorships, which terrorized their own people into submission, were seldom called terrorists. Since World War II, many governments in Africa, Asia, and Latin America have used

terror to keep themselves in power. Between 1973 and 1988, the country of Chile was ruled by a military general, Augusto Pinochet. His dictatorship, like the succession of army-led governments in neighboring Argentina (1969–82), created a climate of fear by kidnapping, killing, and "disappearing" thousands of its opponents.

In Iran, the regime of Ayatollah Khomeini followed a similar policy after 1979, when a revolution occurred that replaced the constitutional monarchy with an Islamic republic. The Argentine military claimed to be "saving the nation," the followers of the Ayatollah to be "saving the revolution." Their opponents claimed that both governments were only really interested in crushing dissent.

▲ A *mujahideen* fighter in Afghanistan in 1987.

International terrorism in peacetime

On September 20, 2001, President George W. Bush told Congress that the War on Terror would not end "until every terrorist group of global reach has been found, stopped, and defeated." The group uppermost in his mind was al-Qaeda, which had just launched the devastating 9/11 attacks on the U.S.

Al-Qaeda is a product of the Afghan civil wars. These began in 1978 as a domestic conflict between communist modernizers and Islamic traditionalists, but in 1979, the Soviet Union intervened on the side of the communists. Eager young men came from all over the Muslim world to fight on the side of the traditionalist guerrillas, the *mujahideen*. After the Soviets were defeated in 1989, many of these young men were keen to continue the fight for Islam in other countries. Two of the men, Osama bin Laden and Abdullah Azzam, set up an office in neighboring Pakistan, recruiting soldiers for all the global conflicts involving Muslims. They called themselves al-Qaeda, or "the Base."

It's a fact

The two founders of al-Qaeda disagreed about tactics. Osama bin Laden favored a major terrorist campaign against the West and its supporters, but Abdullah Azzam was less willing to target civilians, particularly women and children. In November 1989, Azzam was blown up in his car, probably by Egyptian allies of bin Laden.

A global network

During the following decade, many foreign veterans of the Afghan civil wars returned to their own countries. Some went to fight in places such as Chechnya or Kashmir, and others stayed in Afghanistan, running training camps in guerrilla and terrorist techniques for new recruits. A loose global network of Islamic militant groups and individuals was slowly built up. In 1998, al-Qaeda launched its first major terrorist attack, bombing the U.S. embassies in Kenya and Tanzania, killing 227 people. Three years later, almost 3,000 died in the 9/11 attacks.

How did al-Qaeda's leaders seek to justify these murders? They claimed that the Middle East, and in particular its Muslim holy places, was effectively occupied by the U.S. and its allies. In their eyes, this "occupation" was both an insult to Islam and an obstacle to political and economic progress. Though direct military involvement was impossible, they realized that international terrorism could be both possible and effective. A successful attack on the U.S. would show all Muslims that they could strike back.

Opponents of these tactics have two principal arguments. The first is that the deliberate killing of civilians can never be justified. The second is that the only lasting effect of these attacks was the pain they brought to so many families. It is certainly true that the most immediate, deepest, and long-lasting impact of the 9/11 attacks was felt by the families of the victims. However, many observers, both Muslim and non-Muslim, believe that the 9/11 attacks also marked a real turning point in history. This one act of terrorism, they said, had succeeded in changing the world. The fact that terrorism clearly does have an impact—albeit a highly destructive and negative one—is a problem, because it encourages terrorists in their belief, mistaken or otherwise, that these tactics will be effective in helping them achieve their ends.

summary

▶ Some people argue that terrorist tactics can be used successfully in peacetime to change minds and policies, but it is necessary for the political goals to be clearly defined and possible.

▶ Other people argue that terrorist tactics cannot be used successfully in peacetime, because killing civilians is morally wrong, and because they work much too rarely to justify the human cost.

◀ An injured man is removed from the wreckage of the U.S. Embassy in Nairobi on August 7, 1998. Four members of al-Qaeda were later tried and convicted for this bombing.

CHAPTER 4

Counterterrorism and civil liberties

In the fight against terrorism, governments can sometimes act in ways that infringe the human rights of individuals and groups. These are the rights that most people believe should be enjoyed by everyone. They include the right to say and write what we please, the right to live in privacy, and the right not to be arrested without due legal process. For people living in democratic countries, these all sound like very reasonable things to expect, and most of the time they are.

However, a problem can arise when these human rights conflict with the duty of a government to protect its citizens—for

▼ Hundreds of people gather in Boston, Massachusetts, in 2003. They are protesting at what they perceive to be an erosion of civil liberties by the U.S. government following the events of 9/11.

example, when it is under threat from a terrorist attack. Or, to put it another way, the rights of individuals who are suspected of terrorism must be set against the right of every other citizen not to be killed in a terrorist attack.

Governments must try to strike a balance between these competing interests. In the wake of a serious terrorist attack, governments are often tempted to put the needs of national security above those of individual human rights. They may pass laws that limit certain freedoms. This may lead to accusations that the government is using a perceived terrorist threat—or even exaggerating that threat—in order to increase government and police powers at the expense of human rights. The rights that are most often affected by counterterrorist legislation are the right to free speech, privacy, and access to justice.

Free speech

Publicity is crucial to any terrorist campaign. One reason why terrorists commit such high-profile acts of carnage is to attract publicity to their cause. They can also achieve this aim through speeches, written articles, and films. In 1988, in an attempt to deny terrorists publicity, the U.K. government banned the broadcasting of the voices of leaders of Irish terrorist organizations, most notably Gerry Adams, a political spokesman for the IRA. The ban was criticized by human rights organizations around the world and by members of the British media. Many argued that the ban merely increased interest in Adams and others. Better, they said, to hear their words, however abhorrent most people might find them, so that their arguments can be challenged in free and open debate.

Following 9/11, no such heavy-handed measures were imposed to limit free speech. The reason for this may have been that the vast majority of people were so horrified by the attacks that little, if any, airtime was likely to be given to supporters of al-Qaeda on the mainstream media. The U.S. administration's declaration of a War on Terror was also generally accepted by the media, particularly in the U.S., as were later assertions that anyone criticizing this war was helping the enemy.

In the U.S., some schoolteachers who questioned elements of their government's response to 9/11 found themselves accused of lacking patriotism. Also, when Al Jazeera, the Arab TV station, broadcast videotapes from Osama bin Laden, the U.S. tried, unsuccessfully, to have the station censored.

viewpoints

"Democratic nations must try to find ways to starve the terrorist . . . of the oxygen of publicity on which they depend."
British Prime Minister Margaret Thatcher, speaking to the American Bar Association, July 1985 (the ABA represents the legal profession)

"It is easy to defend freedom of speech when the message is something many people find at least reasonable. But the defense of freedom of speech is most critical when the message is one most people find repulsive."
American Civil Liberties Union statement, December 14, 2001

In the U.K., some Islamic clerics spoke out in support of al-Qaeda's basic aims. The government eventually responded in 2006, by making it an offense to "glorify" terrorism. Supporters of this measure argued that allowing the encouragement of terrorism was both foolish and dangerous. Opponents claimed that free speech was being compromised for no good reason.

Privacy

Many terrorist organizations operate as secret cells both within and outside the country they are attacking. Consequently it is usually quite difficult to expose them through ordinary police activity. Intelligence services are therefore often used to spy on suspects in order to collect evidence of their involvement in terrorist activities. Various surveillance methods are used, including telephone tapping, tracking email and internet usage, and checking computer hard drives and personal records.

All of these involve infringements of the suspects' right to privacy. Governments argue, and most people accept, that when people's lives are at risk from a terrorist plot, a certain infringement of this right is justifiable. The British civil liberties group Liberty has actually argued in favor of the use of telephone-tapping evidence in court. They say this is preferable to obtaining evidence by holding suspects in detention for long periods without trial. However, it is easy to see how the power of a government to spy on its citizens can be abused.

After 9/11, the U.S. Patriot Act was passed (October 2001), giving sweeping new powers to the intelligence and security agencies, including powers that affected the right of privacy. The law made it easier to arrest, detain, and seize the property of anyone suspected of involvement in terrorist acts. Suspects could also have their email and internet usage tracked, their phones tapped, and their financial, medical and educational records examined. In November 2002, the U.S. Department of Defense announced a new system for tracking personal information called Total Information Awareness. This used the

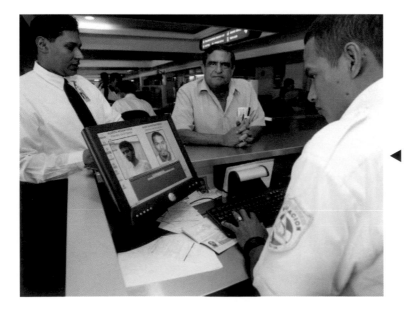

◀ In May 2005, an immigration officer at Nicaragua's international airport has the faces of two al-Qaeda suspects on his information screen. Is this type of surveillance an acceptable way to protect public safety, or an attack on the personal freedoms of the people concerned?

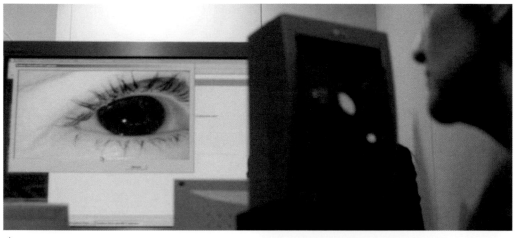

▲ A U.K. Home Office minister (official) is given a demonstration of how retina scans can be used on personal identity cards.

global computer network to search through credit card records, passport applications, and sales of relevant items such as airline tickets and guns.

In the U.K., the November 2001 Antiterrorism Crime and Security Act contained many measures similar to those included in the U.S. Patriot Act. The British government also announced that it would be introducing personal identity cards, at least in part as a weapon against terrorism. These cards would contain proof of individual identity and other, as yet unspecified, personal details.

All these American and British measures represented potential invasions of privacy. The two governments argued that the War on Terror made them necessary, that if terrorists were to be caught, then the intelligence and security services needed all the information they could get. And if that meant a reduction in the right to personal privacy, then such a sacrifice was clearly worthwhile. The British government pointed

out that identity cards had long been accepted in many European democracies. Many people accepted this reasoning, but others were less convinced. Some critics accepted that a slight reduction in civil liberties might be necessary for a successful campaign against terrorism, but still thought that their governments were going too far. Others feared that some governments would simply use the War on Terror as an excuse for restricting the liberties of their internal opponents.

▲ A protest against internment in Northern Ireland takes place outside the British Parliament building in London in 1971. Many of the demonstrators were relatives of people who had been imprisoned without trial.

Access to justice

Access to justice is a fundamental right in all countries that respect the rule of law. It includes the right not to be unlawfully detained, the right to know the reasons for the detention, the right to legal counsel, and to a fair trial within a reasonable time. These rights are generally observed in democratic countries. However, governments sometimes feel under pressure to disregard some or all of these rights in cases of suspected terrorists, particularly at times when a country feels under threat from terrorism.

In August 1971, in the wake of a series of terrorist attacks across Northern Ireland, the British government introduced *internment*, the incarceration without trial of suspected terrorists in prison camps. Internment continued until December 1975, and during that period over 1,900 people were detained without receiving a trial. The policy was supported by many

in the Protestant community, who believed this was the only way of dealing with the IRA threat. However, it attracted widespread criticism across Britain, because it appeared to target almost exlusively Catholic suspects. It also failed to stop terrorism, and provoked a campaign of civil disobedience by the Catholic community of Northern Ireland.

The climate of fear that led to internment in 1971 was felt once again on a much broader scale 30 years later after the 9/11 attacks. The U.S. Patriot Act and U.K. Antiterrorism Crime and Security Act made it easier for the authorities to arrest those suspected of involvement in terrorism. Noncitizens, in particular, were denied access to justice. They could now be held indefinitely without charge or trial, or deported with little or no chance of challenging the decision effectively. In some countries, such as India, these harsh measures applied to citizens as well.

Critics claim that permitting detention without charge or trial crucially undermines the rule of law. Indefinite detention is cruel, they say, and likely to be counterproductive. Most of those detained are Muslims, and they may be regarded as martyrs, encouraging sympathy from their community and causing further disaffection with Western society.

Supporters of the new rules claim that many of those arrested around the world present a clear danger to their societies. If there is insufficient evidence to try and convict them, they say, then it seems safer to keep them locked up than risk releasing potential terrorists back into the society. Some innocent people may be detained unnecessarily, but many more may suffer if a determined terrorist is set free.

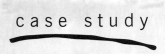

case study

Abu Hamza al-Masri

The radical Muslim cleric, Abu Hamza al-Masri, was born in Egypt in 1958 and moved to Britain in 1979. In 1997, he installed himself as leader of the Finsbury Park Mosque in north London and soon became notorious for his hate-filled speeches against Jews, homosexuals, women, and others. On the first anniversary of 9/11, Hamza co-organized a conference at the mosque praising the hijackers. In January 2003, the mosque was closed by police, but Hamza, still free, preached outside its gates. In October 2005, he was charged with 15 U.K. offenses, and, in February 2006, was found guilty of 11 of them, including inciting murder and stirring up racial hatred. He was jailed for seven years. Should the British authorities have acted sooner to arrest Abu Hamza? Many people, including Muslims, were shocked that he had been left free to preach his messages of intolerance for so long.

▲ Abu Hamza, the Muslim cleric, leads prayers outside the North London Central Mosque in the U.K., April 2004.

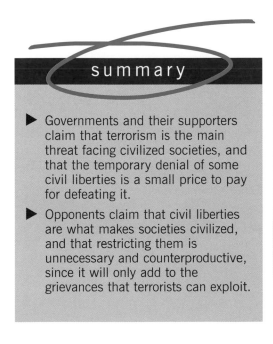

summary

▶ Governments and their supporters claim that terrorism is the main threat facing civilized societies, and that the temporary denial of some civil liberties is a small price to pay for defeating it.

▶ Opponents claim that civil liberties are what makes societies civilized, and that restricting them is unnecessary and counterproductive, since it will only add to the grievances that terrorists can exploit.

CHAPTER 5

Terrorism and international law

Domestic law regulates relations between citizens within a state. International law chiefly regulates relations between states. It is, however, compulsory for citizens to obey domestic laws, whereas states can, and often do, choose to ignore international laws. There is no universally accepted world government or world court to enforce them. The United Nations (UN) can punish some international law-breakers, but only when all the members of the Security Council vote in agreement. Since the most powerful states have the right to veto Security Council decisions, this means that they and their allies are essentially above the law.

International law, though a weak instrument, remains important in the fight against terrorism and as a means of governing states' responses to terrorist attacks. International law has played a prominent role in four areas: cross-border conflicts between states and terrorist groups; the treatment of foreign terrorist suspects; state-sponsored terrorism; and targeted killings of foreign terrorist suspects.

Cross-border conflicts

International laws to regulate relations between states work reasonably well so long as states are the main international participants. When the forces of state A cross the borders of state B, for example, it is fairly clear that an international law has been broken, that state A has broken it, and state B has the right to retaliate. However, in today's "globalized" world,

 The United Nations Security Council in session on March 27, 2006.

where states share the international stage with huge business corporations and international terrorist organizations, things are not so clear. If state A is attacked by a terrorist organization whose headquarters are located in state B, does state A have the right to attack state B?

For example, in 2006, a war was fought between Israel and Hezbollah, a powerful, radical Islamic movement based within Lebanon. The conflict began on July 12, when Hezbollah fired rockets at Israeli border villages, then kidnapped two Israeli soldiers and killed three more. Israel responded with massive artillery fire and airstrikes against suspected Hezbollah targets within Lebanon, damaging the Lebanese infrastructure. More than 1,400 people were killed in a month-long conflict, most of them Lebanese civilians. A UN-brokered ceasefire came into effect on August 14.

So, was Lebanon legally responsible for the actions taken by Hezbollah? According to international law, it does not matter whether the soldiers are part of the regular forces of a state or not—if an attack is launched by, or on behalf of, that state, it is regarded as an armed attack by that state. It has been argued that since Hezbollah forms part of the Lebanese government, the Lebanese government

should hold at least partial responsibility for the attack. Yet the Lebanese government denied responsibility for the attack and called for UN intervention to end the conflict. The question of the Lebanese state's responsibility is therefore open to debate.

viewpoints

"Hezbollah is part of the Lebanese government and acts of Hezbollah can well be considered to be those of the Lebanese Government, notwithstanding that the Christian elements in the government have categorically disassociated themselves from the Hezbollah attack."
Dr. Robbie Sabel of the Hebrew University Faculty of Law in Jerusalem, Israel, quoted on July 27, 2006

"The [Lebanese] government was not aware of, and does not take responsibility for, nor endorses what happened on the international border."
Lebanese Prime Minister Fouad Siniora, speaking about the Hezbollah attack, quoted on July 12, 2006

A man walks through the ▶ ruins of a factory in Haifa, Israel, which was hit by a Hezbollah rocket attack on July 23, 2006.

▲ Lebanese men survey the rubble in the southern suburbs of Beirut following an Israeli air attack on August 12, 2006.

Israel's right to attack Lebanon has also been questioned. Israel claimed that the Lebanese government had refused (or was unable) to carry out an earlier UN resolution to disarm Hezbollah. Israel argued that it therefore had the right to take action against Hezbollah in retaliation for its rocket attacks, even though Hezbollah was on Lebanese territory. According to international law, if a state fails to prevent armed bands in its territory from attacking a neighboring state, the neighboring state is entitled to defend itself against those armed bands.

The treatment of foreign terrorist suspects

The status of imprisoned foreign terrorist suspects is not clearly defined in international law. They do not, for example, have the status of prisoners of war (POWs), as would apply to combatants captured during a conventional war. According to the Geneva Convention, POWs have the same legal rights as members of the armed forces of the country that is imprisoning them, including the right to legal counsel, the right to call witnesses, and the right of appeal. Countries often take advantage of the

uncertainty regarding the legal status of terrorist suspects to deny them such rights.

For example, in November 2003, Maher Arar, a Canadian-Syrian national, claimed he had been tortured in a Syrian prison after having been handed over to the Syrian authorities by the U.S. for alleged terrorist offences. Also, in the U.K., between 2001 and 2005, 17 foreign nationals were held without trial under the Antiterrorism, Crime, and Security Act. The U.K. government defended this action, saying the prisoners constituted a security threat. However, the House of Lords ruled in 2004 that indefinite imprisonment without charge or trial was incompatible with European human rights laws.

During and since the 2001 invasion of Afghanistan, military, security, and police forces around the world have arrested around 70,000 suspected terrorists. Most have since been released; but an unknown number are still held by the forces that arrested them. Around 700 were either arrested by, or handed over to, the U.S. government. These were imprisoned in Camp X-Ray, a purpose-built detention center in the U.S. naval base at Cuba's Guantanamo Bay.

The treatment of War on Terror prisoners has been complicated by the very idea of a "war" on terrorism. If this was a war in the traditional sense of a conflict between states, then things would be simple—the international laws and conventions on the treatment of POWs would apply. Their movement would be restricted, but they would not be interrogated. They would be fed and housed until the conflict was over. If, on the other hand, this is viewed not as a war, but as an international campaign against terrorism, different rules would apply. Terrorist acts are crimes wherever they are committed, and terrorists would be treated simply as criminals. They would then be given those rights normally accorded to criminals in a free society: legal representation, trial, and—if found guilty—a clear sentence.

President Bush's government argued that the detainees were neither POWs nor criminals, and were not entitled to the rights of either. A new category was created for them—that of "enemy combatants." In a war that had no foreseeable or likely end, they could be held and interrogated for as long as the authorities wanted, and denied rights to legal representation or trial. In June 2004, the U.S. Supreme Court ruled that such denials were illegal.

It's a fact

President Bush's government has not tried to justify torture of terror suspects, which is prohibited by U.S. law. There is evidence to suggest, however, that U.S. intelligence agencies have flown terror suspects to countries where torture is routinely practiced—like Egypt, Morocco, and Uzbekistan—for interrogation. This process is called *extraordinary rendition*.

▼ Orange jump-suited arrivals at the Guantanamo detention facility in Cuba await "processing" under the watchful eyes of U.S. military police in January 2002.

Those people who agree with the detention of terrorist suspects without trial argue that it is necessary in the fight against terrorism. They say that such people are too dangerous to release, and that there is often insufficient evidence to try them in court. They claim that continued interrogations help uncover terrorist networks, lead to further arrests, and ultimately save lives. Opponents claim that many innocent people are held without hope of release, and that the rule of law and the United States' image abroad are being seriously undermined.

State-sponsored terrorism

Some countries arm and fund terrorist organizations as a means of launching attacks against their (the countries') enemies without any outward sign of their involvement. This practice, known as state-sponsored terrorism, is not easily dealt with under international law. In ordinary circumstances, if a terrorist act is committed on foreign soil, the country in which the suspected terrorist lives is obliged, under international law, to prosecute the suspect. Alternatively, the suspect may be sent to the country that

was attacked for prosecution there (known as *extradition*). However, if the suspect was sponsored by the state in which he or she lives, then that state can hardly be relied upon to provide a fair trial.

An example of this nature arose after the bombing of Pan Am flight 103, which exploded over Lockerbie, Scotland, in December 1988, killing 270 people. The suspected terrorists were Libyan nationals, and the Libyan government declared that it would prosecute the suspects in its own courts. But investigators had uncovered evidence that the Libyan government itself had sponsored the bombing. Most of the fatalities were British and U.S. citizens, and the governments of both countries, supported by a UN Security Council resolution, insisted that Libya extradite the suspects to either the U.K. or U.S. for prosecution. Libya's refusal to do so led to the UN imposing sanctions on the country. In 1999, the suspects were finally extradited to a neutral country (the Netherlands), then tried and sentenced under Scottish law.

This example suggests that terrorist suspects cannot be tried in the state that sponsored their activities. But should they

◀ Scottish rescue workers inspect the wreckage of the stricken Pan Am flight 103 in a field east of the town of Lockerbie, Scotland, in December 1988.

be tried in the targeted state instead? Some international law experts argue that foreign terrorist suspects cannot be expected to receive a fair trial in the state that was the target of their attack, because public and media pressure may prejudice the trial's outcome. They say that it would be better for such trials to take place at the International Criminal Court (ICC). However, it is likely that for the foreseeable future targeted states will insist on trying foreign terrorist suspects themselves.

Retaliation

In many cases, a criminal prosecution of a terrorist suspect is not feasible, and targeted countries may choose to respond to an attack in other ways. This may include taking military action against the state that sponsored the attack. For example, in 1986, after two U.S. soldiers were killed by a bomb in a West Berlin disco, investigations revealed that the perpetrators had been trained in Libya. The U.S. government launched air strikes on a number of targets in Libya, including suspected terrorist training facilities, killing more than 100 people. Were the attacks legal? Under international law, armed force is prohibited unless a border has been crossed and a nation is under direct attack, or when the UN Security Council has sanctioned it. President Ronald Reagan argued that American citizens had been under direct attack in this instance, and the U.S. was exercising its right to self-defense under Article 51 of the UN Charter. Most international law experts disagreed, saying this was a retaliatory attack rather than one of self-defense.

It's a fact

When individuals or groups are targeted in air strikes, innocent civilians often share the fate of the intended targets. Those launching the strikes often express regret for what they call "collateral damage," but refuse to accept any moral responsibility for the civilian deaths. Critics argue that if deaths of this kind are to be expected, then such strikes are effectively targeting civilians, and can be considered terrorist acts.

viewpoints

"The prosecution of [state-sponsored] terrorism cases to date is pursued at the national level, largely in the targeted State. Given the underlying factors shaping this practice, this arrangement, as imperfect as it is, likely will, and quite probably should, remain in place for the foreseeable future."
Madeline Morris, professor of law, Duke Law School, Durham, North Carolina.

"In light of the tragic events of September 11, 2001 . . . there may never be a greater opportunity or greater political will to expand the jurisdiction of the envisaged ICC to include the crime of terrorism and to provide a forum for civil claims arising from acts of state-sponsored terrorism."
William P. Hoye, associate vice president, deputy general counsel, and concurrent associate professor of law, University of Notre Dame, Indiana.

In 1998, the remains of a U.S. cruise missile are inspected following the bombing of a factory in Khartoum, Sudan.

International law also forbids preemptive strikes against terrorists or their sponsors. Yet states have occasionally practiced this. In 1998, following the bombing of the two U.S. embassies in East Africa, President Clinton ordered missile attacks on a factory in the Sudanese capital, Khartoum. Intelligence claimed that the factory was producing chemical weapons that might be used against U.S. targets. In fact, it was manufacturing medicines. In 2003, President Bush and British Prime Minister Tony Blair decided that intelligence reports of Iraqi weapons of mass destruction (WMD) justified an invasion of Iraq. In fact, no WMD were ever found. The war and subsequent violence in Iraq have cost more than 100,000 civilian lives.

What if the intelligence had been right? Would that have justified preemptive attacks in breach of international law? Supporters of preemptive strikes say yes, that winning the War on Terror is more important than obeying outdated laws. Opponents argue that laws cannot simply be discarded when they become inconvenient.

Targeted killings

In the fight against terrorism, states have sometimes resorted to targeted killings—that is, the elimination of individuals whom they regard as responsible for terrorist attacks. Israel has frequently used this method against members of Palestinian militant groups, and have carried out some 80 attacks between 2001 and 2006.

Is there a justification for this kind of action in international law? If the attacks take place on foreign soil, they can be considered a violation of sovereignty, unless authorized by the nation in which the operation takes place. However, in wartime a different code of international law applies, known as the Law of Armed Conflict (LOAC). Two principles of the LOAC apply in the case of targeted killings: distinction and proportionality. Distinction requires the perpetrators to distinguish between combatants and noncombatants, and proportionality states that destruction of lives and property must be proportional to the military advantage gained.

Supporters claim that targeted killings are necessary. The targets, who are wanted for old terrorist crimes or suspected of planning new ones, cannot be arrested. Either they live in inaccessible places, or the local government is unable or unwilling to arrest them. So killing them is the only way of preventing them from killing others. Opponents say that targeted killings are a form of state terrorism.

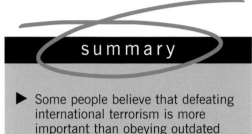

summary

▶ Some people believe that defeating international terrorism is more important than obeying outdated laws. International laws were written to regulate relations between states, and are an obstacle to those involved in the fight against terrorist groups.

▶ Other people believe that international laws may have to be changed—by international agreement—to meet the new challenge of terrorism, but breaking them unilaterally weakens respect for both law-breaker and laws.

case study

Qaed Salim Sinan al-Harethi

On November 3, 2002, Qaed Salim Sinan al-Harethi may or may not have been al-Qaeda's chief operative in Yemen. U.S. intelligence said he was, and that he had planned the suicide bombing of the destroyer U.S.S. *Cole* in Yemeni waters two years earlier.

On that November day, al-Harethi's car was driving down a remote highway in Yemen when it was hit by an U.S. Hellfire missile that had been fired from a pilotless Predator drone. Al-Harethi and his five companions were all killed.

How could the attack be justified? The two countries were at peace, so the killing could not be considered an act of war. No arrest had been attempted, no trial held, or verdict pronounced. "The president has made it clear that we fight the war on terrorism wherever we need," said the White House spokesman, Ari Fleischer. "Terrorists," he added, "don't recognize any borders or nations." The Swedish foreign minister disagreed. He called the killing of al-Harethi "a summary execution that violates human rights."

◀ A U.S. Air Force Predator drone aircraft stands on the landing strip at Kandahar airfield in southern Afghanistan.

CHAPTER 6

The impact of the War on Terror

Since the terrorist attacks of September 11, 2001, the Western powers have commited themselves to a War on Terror. This war has been waged using military force as well as more covert forms of action, such as blocking sources of terrorist finance and putting diplomatic pressure on countries that sponsor terrorism.

By the end of September 2001, it was established that al-Qaeda had been responsible for the attacks. The U.S. assembled a broad coalition to take the fight to the terrorists. The first task of the coalition was to invade Afghanistan, where al-Qaeda was based, with the aim of

It's a fact

The old Soviet Union had enormous civil and military nuclear industries. When it broke up in 1991, the materials and technical expertise used by these industries were scattered across more than a dozen states. Keeping them out of terrorist hands was a difficult job, one that could only be done with the help of the Russian and other post-Soviet intelligence services.

▼ Soldiers of the Afghan Northern Alliance: they and their comrades bore the brunt of the ground war against the Taliban in October and November 2001.

toppling the Taliban regime and destroying al-Qaeda's terrorist training camps in the eastern part of the country.

Help from dictators

When the decision had been taken to invade Afghanistan, the U.S. and its allies sought the support of neighboring Pakistan. That country was far from a democracy, and its intelligence service, the PSI, had played a crucial role in helping the Taliban to power in Afghanistan. What mattered now, however, was ensuring that the invasion of Afghanistan proved successful. The use of Pakistani airfields and airspace would make the invasion easier, and Pakistani assistance in blocking the border with Afghanistan would make it more difficult for the al-Qaeda and Taliban leaders to escape.

Intelligence failures

Since the successful invasion of Afghanistan in 2001, two types of failure have threatened to undermine the War on Terror. The first type involves government—either the failure of a central government to control all its territory or the complete disappearance of any central authority. Such failed states provide the ideal sanctuary for terrorist groups, who can seize a particular area and set up training facilities in relative safety. Those carrying out the War on Terror then have a choice—to ignore the situation, to attempt to repair the state in question, or to aid other groups in the area. The first option is risky, the second usually too expensive in money and soldiers, so the third has often been chosen. In Afghanistan, the warlords of the Northern Alliance were used to fight against al-Qaeda and the Taliban. In Somalia, local warlords have also been supported against incoming terrorist groups.

▲ In Somalia, militiamen such as these have long been involved in power struggles between different warring factions. Terrorist groups find it relatively easy to set up their operations in embattled states like this.

The other type of failure that has threatened to undermine the War on Terror is a failure of coordination between the world's intelligence and security services. The successful pursuit of terrorists is only possible when there are no gaping holes in the international net. The West needed Russian help, for example, because the cooperation of the security network in the ex-Soviet countries was essential for tracking both terrorists and potential WMD. It was not surprising, therefore, that Western governments chose to focus on Chechen terrorist outrages like the 2002 Moscow theater siege and the 2004 Beslan school siege, rather than criticize the Russian government for its human rights violations in Chechnya.

Hidden agendas

Until January 29, 2002, it was widely assumed that the War on Terror was aimed at international terrorist groups in general and at al-Qaeda in particular. On that day, President Bush announced a widening of the war to include states either sponsoring terrorism, producing weapons of mass destruction, or both. Iran, Iraq, and North Korea were named. They and others, he said, made up an "Axis of Evil."

In the past, Iran has given weapons and financial support to the Hezbollah group in southern Lebanon, which uses terrorist tactics against Israel. Under Saddam Hussein, Iraq offered money to the relatives of Palestinian suicide bombers. North Korea had no record of supporting terrorism, but was hostile to the U.S. and was believed to be trying to develop nuclear weapons. It appeared that none of these had any connection to al-Qaeda, though all three considered themselves enemies of the U.S.

Invasion

The Bush Administration's foreign policy, which had been drawn up by neoconservatives in the mid-1990s, called for vigorous action against any state that threatened U.S. interests or dominance. Many observers believe that the Bush Administration was pursing just such a neoconservative agenda when it led the invasion of Iraq in 2003. They claim its main motives for the invasion had little to do with the War on Terror and much more to do with protecting U.S. interests in the region, including securing access to Iraq's oil, setting up military bases, and establishing an Iraqi "beacon of democracy" for the Middle East. The War on Terror, the critics said, had been used as a cover.

summary

▶ Supporters of the current War on Terror say that it should be waged against terrorist groups and governments who support them. All governments who say they are fighting terrorism should be supported.

▶ Opponents of the current War on Terror say it is being lost because the original focus on international terrorist groups has been abandoned, and that widening the war to include other (mostly Muslim) enemies only creates new grievances and terrorists.

case study

The War in Iraq

In March 2003, a U.S.-led coalition invaded Iraq. The attack was presented as part of the War on Terror. Saddam Hussein's government, it was alleged, had connections to al-Qaeda and was developing weapons of mass destruction. Iraq also stood in breach of numerous UN resolutions calling on it to destroy its WMD, and had repeatedly refused to let UN officials inspect its weapons stocks.

The al-Qaeda and WMD allegations turned out to be false, however. There *had* been contact between al-Qaeda and Iraq, but no cooperation; and although most of the international community was convinced that Saddam's regime had been developing WMD during the 1990s, no WMD were found in Iraq.

The occupation of Iraq provoked resistance, and terrorist tactics were increasingly used against the occupation forces. The Bush Administration subsequently claimed that defeating the resistance would be a victory in the War on Terror. Opponents pointed out that the invasion had supplied the terrorists with a new cause and a new battlefield, and had made the war much harder to win. In September 2006, an intelligence assessment released by the White House confirmed that this was indeed the case.

◀ Months after the end of the war in Iraq, U.S. soldiers struggle to maintain order. Meanwhile the Iraqi people suffer from water and electricity shortages and wait in long lines to buy basic necessities for survival.

CHAPTER 7

Terrorism in the twenty-first century

Terrorism has changed a great deal in recent decades. In the early twenty-first century, the most potent terrorist threat comes from Islamic fundamentalism, while the threat from nonreligious political or nationalist terrorism has diminished.

The structure and methods of terrorist organizations have also changed. Today, organizations such as al-Qaeda have evolved into a loose network of secret cells and affiliated groups in many parts of the world. They are adept at using the global banking system and the internet to transfer funds, communicate with members, attract new recruits, disseminate propaganda, and coordinate attacks. It is likely that this way of operating will grow more and more sophisticated as the century progresses.

New methods

Suicide bombing has become the most widely used tactic among Islamist terrorists. Another gruesome modern development is the execution of kidnapped civilians or members of the military, usually by beheading. This is often filmed and then broadcast on the internet as a means of spreading fear and raising the profile of a particular terrorist group.

It is possible that in the future terrorist groups will get hold of weapons of mass

viewpoints

"Millennial Islamism is an ideology [a set of views] superimposed upon a religion— illusion upon illusion. It is not merely violent in tendency. Violence is all that is there."
Martin Amis, the *Observer* (U.K.), September 10, 2006

"The global war on terror is a smokescreen used by governments to wipe out opponents."
Headline in the *Guardian* (U.K.), August 28, 2003

◄ Iraqi policemen stand next to a blown-up minibus in central Baghdad. Since the invasion, suicide bombings have become a regular occurrence in the Iraqi capital.

▲ The future of terrorism? Post office workers are led to a decontamination unit following an anthrax scare at a main postal sorting office in Liverpool, U.K., in October 2001.

summary

▶ Governments should take action against any terrorist group or failed state that threatens their safety and security.

▶ In the fight against terrorism, the West should resist labeling all political violence as terrorism. It should define more carefully who its real enemies are, and target them. Otherwise it could end up fighting on too many fronts.

destruction, including nuclear, biological, and chemical weapons. Such weapons have already been used on occasion. In October 2001, spores of the bacterial disease anthrax were sent via the U.S. postal service to several senators and media figures.

Counterterrorism

As terrorism grows more sophisticated, counterterrorist agencies will need to adapt. Resources will need to be targeted effectively, and in order to do this, people will need to agree on what terrorism is. Since the events of 9/11, governments have tended to condemn all politically inspired violence as terrorism. This is understandable, but it is also confusing. After all, political violence against brutal regimes is sometimes justifiable. Some people argue that lumping together all enemies of the "powers that be" in one group makes it harder to concentrate on the most serious threat and can be counterproductive. As most experts now agree, the removal of Saddam Hussein has strengthened al-Qaeda.

Nations need to work with each other and with international bodies to combat terrorism. Intelligence agencies need to pool their knowledge of terrorist networks; governments must act together with the global banking system to freeze bank accounts and block sources of terrorist finance. Governments also need to reorganize their defenses to take account of the new threat to their towns and cities. In the future, governments may need to spend as much on civil protection as on their armed forces.

Finally, it is important to ask ourselves what the best tactics are for dealing with terrorism. Perhaps strong-arm methods are not the most effective. For example, invading countries such as Iraq alienates large numbers of people and potentially creates more terrorist recruits. Terrorism is likely to be with us for as long as there are groups in society who feel oppressed, excluded, or ignored. But whether it remains a major threat to global stability may depend to a large extent on how we decide to confront it today.

Glossary

Biological weapons Weapons using viruses or bacteria found in nature.

Chechens Inhabitants of Chechnya, a small border region in southern Russia.

Chemical weapons Weapons using manmade poisons.

Civil liberties Those freedoms of action and speech which are considered necessary for the proper functioning of a democratic society.

Civil war War between different groups within one country.

Cleric Clergyman or priest.

Coercion Compelling someone to do something by use of force.

Cold War The hostility that existed between the capitalist and the communist worlds between 1947 and the late-1980s.

Collaborators People who work for, or with, an occupying power.

Collateral damage People killed or property destroyed in attacks aimed at other people or property.

Communist A follower of communism, a political theory and practice that in theory puts the interests of society as a whole above the interests of individuals.

Conventions Generally accepted rules.

Counterproductive Having the opposite effect to that intended.

Ethnic Relating to different tribal/racial groups.

Geneva Convention An international agreement first signed at Geneva, Switzerland, in 1864, and later revised, governing the status and treatment of captured soldiers and civilians in wartime.

Guerrilla warfare War fought on one side by unofficial and irregular troops.

Incitement Stirring up.

Inefficacy Ineffectiveness.

Intelligence and security services Secret agencies that seek out information and try to counter enemies, both in their own countries and abroad.

Intimidation Causing fear, often through violence or threats of violence.

Islamic militants Muslims who believe that Islam should play a greater role in the way their society works, and that duty calls them to defend the Islamic world from Western influence.

Left-wing Describing a radical or reforming individual or group.

Neoconservative Literally, "new conservative." In the U.S., the term is used to describe politicians who believe that their country should aggressively make the most of its position as the world's only superpower.

Noncombatant Someone who is not involved in the fighting.

Preemptive attack An attack on an enemy by someone who thinks the enemy is about to attack him or her.

Propaganda The promotion of ideas, often involving a selective version of the truth.

Resistance Fighting against a government that is unwanted because it represents a foreign power or only a narrow section of society.

Sanctuary A place of safety.

Senate The upper assembly of the United States Congress.

Sovereign state An independent country.

Special forces Small groups of soldiers with special skills.

Taliban An Islamic extremist group that ruled most of Afghanistan from 1996 to 2001.

United Nations An international body set up in 1945 to promote peace and cooperation between states.

UN Security Council A council within the UN responsible for the maintenance of world peace and security. It has five permanent members—the U.S., Russia, Britain, France, and China.

Veto To prevent from happening.

Timeline

1793–4 The French Reign of Terror.

1940–5 Massive bombing of civilian targets in World War II.

1971–5 Internment is practiced by the British government against suspected terrorists in Northern Ireland.

1978–96 Wars in Afghanistan.

1983 Suicide bombing of U.S. Marine barracks in Lebanon.

1986 U.S. government launches air strikes against Libya in retaliation for a terrorist attack.

1987–8 Birth of al–Qaeda.

1988 Bombing of Pan Am flight 103 over Lockerbie, Scotland.

1998 (Feb 23) Al-Qaeda declares war on the Unites States.

(Aug 7) Al-Qaeda bombing of U.S. embassies in Nairobi and Dar es Salaam.

(Aug 20) U.S. reprisal attacks on Afghanistan and Sudan.

2001 (Sep 11) Attacks on New York City and the Pentagon.

(Sep 12) George W. Bush declares War on Terror.

(Oct 7) Operation "Enduring Freedom" begins in Afghanistan.

(Oct 26) U.S. Patriot Act.

2002 (Jan 11) First detainees arrive at Guantanamo Bay.

(Jan 29) George W. Bush delivers "Axis of Evil" speech.

(June 1) George W. Bush announces new "preemptive" strategic doctrine.

(Oct 14) Al-Qaeda Bali bombing kills almost 200 people.

(Oct 23) Chechen rebels mount the Moscow theater siege.

(Nov 5) Predator drone attack in Yemen.

2003 (March 20) Invasion of Iraq.

2004 (March 11) Madrid bombings, believed to have been carried out by al-Qaeda.

2005 (July 7) Four al-Qaeda-trained suicide bombers kill themselves and around 60 others in London.

2001–6 Israel carries out around 80 targeted killings of Palestinian militants.

2006 (Aug) Conflict between Israel and the Lebanese militia group, Hezbollah.

Further information

Books to read:

In the News: Terrorism
Adam Hibbert
(Franklin Watts, 2002)

21st Century Debates: Terrorism – The Impact on our Lives
Alex Woolf
(Wayland, 2005)

Al-Qaeda
Jason Burke
(Penguin, 2004)

Two Hours That Shook the World
Fred Halliday
(Saqi, 2002)

Terrorism: a very short introduction
Charles Townshend
(OUP, 2002)

Due to the changing nature of Internet links, The Rosen Publishing Group, Inc., has developed an online list of Web sites related to the subject of this book. This site is updated regularly. Please use this link to access the list:
www.rosenlinks.com/ed/terror/

Index